Nuttall's
Fabric Facts

COMPILED BY
HELEN PERRIN, B.Sc., M.Sc.

Main Sections
FIBRES AND FABRICS
LAUNDERING
STAIN REMOVAL
DRESSMAKING

FREDERICK WARNE London

CONTENTS

© Frederick Warne & Co. Ltd., England, 1976

ISBN 0 7232 1991 5

Reprinted 1977

Printed in Great Britain by William Clowes & Sons, Limited
London, Beccles and Colchester

2351.877

INTRODUCTION

This book is designed to provide information to help the consumer to achieve the best results from the tremendous range of fabrics and aids for their care available today.

Numerous man-made fibres have been developed in recent years. Fabrics are woven or knitted from these, and from blends of natural and man-made fibres. Similar fabrics may be sold under different brand names, and it is not always clear what the constituent fibres are. The consumer is faced with a bewildering choice. Many of the fibres and fabrics, with alternative names, which are obtainable today are listed in the first chapter of the book, with details of their characteristics and care.

The life of a garment will be extended and its good appearance conserved if it is handled correctly. The chapters on Laundering, Stain Removal and Dressmaking deal with these aspects of fabric care. The wrong action—when a garment is sewn, laundered or treated for stains—will prevent it appearing at its best, and may even damage it, possibly beyond repair. Different fabrics require different treatment, a point which cannot be emphasized too strongly.

Thanks are due to the Home Laundering Consultative Council (HLCC) for permission to reproduce the symbols and instructions for laundering.

FIBRES AND FABRICS

Characteristics and Care

In recent years many man-made fibres have been added to the natural fibres which have been used for clothing and furnishings for thousands of years. These man-made fibres may be used on their own, or combined with other fibres so that the good qualities of one complement those of the other.

There are five main groups of man-made fibres:

Acetates (and **triacetates**) and **viscose** (rayons) which are cellulose based ;

Nylon, polyesters and **acrylics** which are synthetic fibres, made entirely from chemicals.

Fibres within these groups are given many different trade names. The more widely used are included in the following list, along with the natural fibres, some other man-made fibres, fabrics which are blends of fibres, and fabrics known by a special name because of their finish or weave. The characteristics and usages of the fibres and fabrics are listed. General washing and ironing instructions are given, but manufacturers' instructions may differ and should, in that case, be followed. Blends of fibres should be treated according to the weaker fibre, i.e. the one requiring the lower temperature. The washing processes referred to are described in detail in the chapter on **Laundering**. Sewing tips relevant to particular fabrics are included. General sewing information is in the chapter on **Dressmaking**.

Acetate   Well-known brand names for acetate are Dicel and Lansil. It is made from cotton linters or wood pulp, chemically combined with acetic acid. Acetate drapes well, is resilient and absorbent, is resistant to moths and mildew, and dyes easily into a wide range of brilliant shades.

Acetate is employed as an alternative for silk in satins, brocades, etc., and is used for a wide range of clothing as well as lining material, knitting yarns and furnishing fabrics. Avoid oversoiling; wash using process [6/40]. Iron, if necessary, on the reverse side, or over a dry cloth, using a cool iron. Use a padded surface to avoid seam impressions. When sewing, sharp cutting-out scissors are needed, and fine pins and needles. Use a synthetic sewing thread and take care with the machine tension to avoid the seams puckering.

Acrilan Brand name for an acrylic (*q.v.*).

Acrylics Well-known brand names for acrylics are Acrilan, Orlon and Courtelle. They are synthetic fibres produced from acrylonitrile and other chemicals. Acrylics are soft and warm to touch, drape well, are resilient, have low absorbency and are strong, hard-wearing and non-irritant.

They are made up into weaves and knitted fabrics to simulate wool, as well as into knitting yarns and fur fabrics. Acrylic fibres are often used in blends with other fibres, particularly wool. Wash frequently using process [6/40] and press, if necessary, with a cool iron when dry. Treat blends according to the weaker fibre. When sewing, perfect seam tension is essential to avoid puckering seams, and do not stretch the material as it goes through the machine.

Agilon A textured yarn (*q.v.*) made from nylon, Terylene and other man-made fibres.

Antron A brand name for nylon (*q.v.*).

Arnel An American brand name for triacetate (*q.v.*).

Ban-Lon A trade name which identifies garments made from textured yarns (*q.v.*) produced from nylon or certain polyesters.

Bri-Nylon A British brand name for nylon (*q.v.*).

Brocade A fabric with a woven-in pattern, made in silk, viscose, nylon or cotton. Cotton brocades can be washed at home, using process $\boxed{\frac{4}{50}}$. Other brocades should be dry cleaned.

Candlewick Made by inserting tufts of yarn into a woven backing. The tufts are cut to form a pile and the backing fabric is shrunk to lock them in. Candlewick is made from many different fibres, and used for soft furnishings, such as bedspreads, and dressing-gowns. Some candlewick can be machine-washed and wrung (*see* manufacturer's instructions), but otherwise wash by hand using warm water. Care must be taken not to crush the fabric or let it go out of shape. When the candlewick is dry, shake to raise the pile but do not iron.

Celon *see* nylon.

Chiffon A lightweight sheer material made from silk, viscose, nylon or Terylene, used for dresses, blouses, lingerie, scarves, etc. Nylon or Terylene chiffon can be washed using process $\boxed{\frac{6}{40}}$, but silk or viscose chiffon should be dry cleaned. Chiffons are difficult to sew. Tack to tissue paper for support when machining; stitch with a fine needle and small stitches.

Clydella A brand name for a fabric made from 80% cotton and 20% wool. It is strong and warm, but light in weight, and is used for clothing, especially for children and babies. Wash using process $\frac{4}{50}$ and iron when almost dry with a warm iron.

Corduroy A pile fabric with a corded effect, made from cotton or cotton blended with viscose or polyester. Used for clothing, mainly dresses, coats and trousers. Wash using process $\frac{4}{50}$. If necessary press lightly on the wrong side, using a warm iron when almost dry. Cut out and sew as velvet (*q.v.*), though it is easier to handle.

Cotton A natural fibre used for a wide variety of fabrics. Cotton is soft but strong, is absorbent, dyes well and is not weakened by strong sunlight or repeated washing. It can be treated in a number of different ways to increase the easy-care properties (*see* Fabric Finishes, p. 18). It is used for curtains, sheets, dresses and other clothing. Wash using process $\frac{1}{95}$, $\frac{2}{60}$, $\frac{4}{50}$ or $\frac{5}{40}$, depending on the finish and dye fastness. Untreated cotton is improved by the use of starch. Iron when still damp, using a hot iron. Most cottons are very easy to sew.

Courtelle A British brand name for an acrylic fibre (*q.v.*).

Courtolon A textured yarn (*q.v.*) made from nylon.

Crimplene A textured yarn (*q.v.*) made from Terylene [polyester (*q.v.*)]. Used for knitwear and jersey-type fabrics.

Dacron An American polyester fibre (*q.v.*), the equivalent of British Terylene.

Denim Originally a heavy cotton, hard-wearing fabric, but now made in lighter weight for beach wear, jeans, etc., and sometimes blended with viscose. Wash using process $\frac{4}{50}$. Iron when slightly damp; use a hot iron on cotton denim, a cool iron on viscose denim.

Dicel British brand name for an acetate fibre (*q.v.*).

Diolen German brand name for a polyester fibre (*q.v.*).

Dralon German brand name for an acrylic fibre (*q.v.*).

Dynel American brand name for a modacrylic fibre (*q.v.*).

Elastomeric fibre This fibre is made from polyurethane and replaces rubber in stretch fabrics. It is highly elastic, very strong but lightweight. It is used with many fibres as an elastic thread in foundation garments, swimsuits, etc. The washing process to be used depends on the fibre with which the elastomeric fibre is combined. Do not iron.

Enkalon A brand name for viscose (*q.v.*).

Evlan A modified viscose (*q.v.*) developed specifically for carpets; it is hard-wearing and abrasion resistant. It is used on its own or in blends with nylon, wool or Courtelle.

Felt A closely matted collection of wool fibres, used for hats, toy-making, etc. It should not be washed, and even dry cleaning is risky as the article may shrink or pull out of shape. Avoid steam pressing which tends to shrink the fabric.

Fibro A brand name for viscose (*q.v.*).

Flannelette A soft, warm, lightweight, flannel-like, fabric made from cotton, or blends of fibres including viscose. Used for nightdresses, pyjamas and sheets. Highly inflammable unless given a flame-resistant finish.

Fluflon The same as Helanca (*q.v.*).

Fur fabric Material resembling fur can be made from many man-made fibres. Fur fabric is best dry cleaned, although small articles can be washed carefully by hand. Never steam press as this can mat the fabric. Use a 'With Nap' layout for cutting out. Baste seams together before machining as the pieces tend to slip during machining. Use a light tension and a long stitch.

Gaberdine A smooth twill-weave fabric made from cotton, worsted (wool), or blends of these with man-made fibres. It is hard-wearing and used for suits, skirts, etc. It can also be given a showerproof finish and be used for rainwear. Coats, other showerproofed articles and worsteds or blended worsteds should be dry cleaned. Light trousers or skirts can be washed using process $\boxed{\frac{4}{50}}$ and pressed when slightly damp with a warm iron.

Glass fibre A fibre woven from fine glass filaments. It is non-absorbent, holds its shape and is sunlight-, crease- and flame-resistant. It is ideal for curtains, but it is brittle and wears easily on the folds. Wash by hand; do not squeeze or wring. Wipe dry or drip-dry; do not use clothes pegs; do not iron. Sew with a long stitch, loose tension, light pressure, sharp needle. If applying a lining, it should also be of glass fibre.

Hair fabrics These are made from the coats of certain animals. Often, because of the rarity of the animal, they are expensive. Their properties are similar to wool (*q.v.*). Heavy articles such as coats should always be dry cleaned, but small knitted garments can be washed carefully, by hand, following the instructions given for wool.

Helanca A textured yarn (*q.v.*) originally made from nylon, but it is now made from Terylene and similar fibres.

Jersey   An elastic, knitted fabric, nowadays made in wool, cotton, silk, or blends of these with man-made fibres. Wool, silk or viscose jersey should be dry cleaned; otherwise wash using process [6/40] . When cutting out do not stretch the fabric. Stretch side-seams slightly when machining or use a zig-zag stitch, to allow for stretching during wear. Tape shoulder seams. Line skirts and trousers to prevent seating.

Lace   There are many varieties of lace. Nylon or Terylene laces used as trimmings can be washed. Dress fabrics should be dry cleaned. Strong lace, such as that used for curtains, can be washed using process [2/60] . Old or fragile lace should be washed with mild soap in warm water and handled as little as possible. Lace should be made up into simple garments, avoiding centre seams. A lace garment should be completely lined or underlined.

Lamé   *see* metallic yarns.

Lansil   A brand name for an acetate fibre (*q.v.*).

Linen   Made from flax, one of the strongest natural fibres known. A lustrous fabric very suitable for tablecloths, sheets, handkerchiefs, etc. It is also used for clothing, although it creases easily unless blended with polyester and given an anti-crease finish. Before washing, stains and marks should be dealt with (*see* Stain Removal, p. 25). Very dirty linen should be soaked in warm soapy water for 15 minutes before washing. Wash using process [1/95] , [2/60] or [5/40] , depending on finish. Iron with a hot iron while still damp. Linen takes a glaze when ironed, which is attractive on table linen, etc., but the glazing can be avoided on garments by pressing on the wrong side or by protecting with

10

a dry cloth. Linen is easy to sew, but it frays badly and all raw edges must be oversewn.

Lurex   *see* metallic yarns.

Lycra   *see* elastomeric fibres.

Metallic yarns   Modern metallic yarns consist of filaments of aluminium covered with plastic. They come in many brilliant colours, and are untarnishable. They can be knitted or woven, and are used for decorative purposes in dresses, furnishings and other fabrics. They can be dry cleaned or washed, depending on the fabric that they are combined with, but all temperatures above 40°C should be avoided. Use a cool iron. When sewing, check if the fabric has a one-way sheen. If so, a 'With Nap' layout must be used. Use pins only in seam allowance to prevent marring the surface. These fabrics tend to unravel, so raw edges should be oversewn.

Metlon   *see* metallic yarns.

Modacrylics   These fibres are a form of modified acrylic. They are similar to acrylics but not so strong, their outstanding characteristic being non-flammability. They are used for clothing, especially protective clothing and children's nightwear, household textiles, knitting yarn and imitation fur. Wash using process $\boxed{\frac{4}{50}}$. Modacrylics are easily damaged by dry heat so do not iron; if dry cleaning is necessary, special processes must be used. Sew as acrylics (*q.v.*).

Nylon   (Polyamide) There are various types of nylon, usually known by number e.g.: Type 66 (Bri-Nylon, Antron), Type 6 (Celon, Enkalon, Perlon), Type 11 (Rilsan), etc. The different types vary slightly, but they all have the same characteristics of high strength to weight ratio, are soft to the touch, have high elasticity and high abrasion resistance. They dye well and are colour-fast when washed, but are badly affected by prolonged direct sunlight. Nylon is easy to wash and dries quickly; it will last a long time if washed before it gets really dirty. Once dirt has penetrated the fibres, or a stain has been allowed to set, it is almost impossible to get it out without damaging the material.

Nylon is made up into many weaves, including velvets, laces and brushed fabrics. It can be permanently pleated. It can be processed to improve handling and warmth, and is then known as bulked, stretch or textured yarn (*q.v.*). It is blended with many other fibres. Nylon is used for a tremendous range of garments and household articles. It does not burn readily, but some finishes make it flammable. Some nets are treated for flame resistance. White and coloured nylon should be washed separately; wash white nylon using process $\frac{3}{60}$, coloureds using process $\frac{4}{50}$. If necessary use a cool iron when almost dry. Treat blends according to the weaker fibre. Sew as acrylics (*q.v.*).

Orlon An American brand name for an acrylic (*q.v.*).

Perlon German brand name for nylon (*q.v.*).

Polyester Produced from petroleum and its by-products, invented and developed in the United Kingdom where the brand name **Terylene** is virtually synonymous with polyester. Dacron is the equivalent fibre produced in the U.S.A. Polyesters are produced in other countries under other brand names. Crimplene is a textured yarn made of Terylene. The good properties of Terylene are its resistance to abrasion and shrinkage, to sunlight fading, moths and mildew. It is very resilient, easy to wash and quick to dry. It is resistant to chemicals, but may be affected by grease stains if they are allowed to remain in contact. It is non-absorbent and non-elastic. Polyester is subject to static electricity, which is a problem in processing and when it is being worn. This also causes it to attract dirt and fluff.

Polyesters are used for many items of clothing, for sewing threads and household textiles. Fabrics are made from blends of polyesters with other fibres such as wool, cotton and viscose. Terylene wadding is used in quilts and pillows. Wash using process $\boxed{\frac{4}{50}}$. Iron with a cool iron when nearly dry. Treat blends according to the weaker fibre. Sew as acrylics (*q.v.*).

P.V.C. (Polyvinyl chloride) A plastic with many household uses; in one form it is similar to the acrylics and is known as a modified or modacrylic (*q.v.*).

Raycelon Yarn made from viscose (rayon) and Celon (nylon). It has good wearing and easy-care combined with absorbent and anti-static properties. Wash as viscose (*q.v.*).

Rayon *see* viscose.

Rexor *see* metallic yarns.

Sarille A modified viscose (*q.v.*). It is permanently crimped to produce fabrics which look like wool.

Satin Satin has a smooth glossy surface on the right side and a dull back. Originally it was made from pure silk, but modern satins are also made from viscose, polyester, nylon and (the most widely used for dresses) acetate and cotton. Wash according to the constituent fibre. Dress satins and heavy furnishing satins should be dry cleaned.

Sayelle An American brand name for a modacrylic (*q.v.*).

Silk   Silk is a luxurious fabric, with a good lustre. It drapes well and is soft and warm. Silk can be 'weighted' to give a larger amount of material without impairing the strength. This material is described as 'silk' or 'all silk'. 'Pure silk' implies that this weighting has not been done. Wild silk (tussore, shantung) consists of silk from caterpillars other than the silkworm. Spun silk is produced from silk waste. ('Artificial silk' is the now obsolete term that was at one time applied to all man-made fabrics.)

Weighted silks have a tendency to water-mark and can also be difficult to iron. They should be dry cleaned. Other silks can be washed using process $\boxed{\frac{7}{40}}$ or $\boxed{\frac{8}{30}}$. Iron wild silk when dry, other silks when slightly damp; use a warm iron on the wrong side of the material. When sewing, use a fine needle and a pure silk thread. Make up light silks with an underlining of Tricel or viscose taffeta.

Spandex   An American name for an elastomeric fibre (*q.v.*).

Spanzelle   British brand name for an elastomeric fibre (*q.v.*).

Spinlene   Scandinavian brand name for a polyester (*q.v.*).

Taffeta   A crisp fabric with a dull sheen originally made from silk, but now made from several fibres including wool, viscose, nylon, acetate and polyester. Wash as the constituent fibre, except for silk and 'watered' taffetas, which should be dry cleaned.

Teklan   British brand name for a modacrylic (*q.v.*).

Tergal, Terital, Terlenka, Terylene, Tetoron and **Trevira**   Brand names for polyester (*q.v.*).

Textured yarns   Some man-made fibres, in particular Terylene and nylon, can be treated by processes known as crimping or high bulking or stretch twisting, which give extreme lightness, bulkiness and elasticity. Textured yarns are used for socks, stockings and tights, stretch underwear, swimsuits and sweaters. Wash frequently, treating according to the constituent fibre. Take care that the article does not become distorted; in particular do not hang up to dry when very wet. When sewing, the remarks made for jersey fabrics apply, because of the similar stretch properties. But some textured yarns tend to unravel, so raw edges must be oversewn.

Triacetate   Known in the United Kingdom as **Tricel**. This fibre is made from wood pulp or cotton linters and oil, and is a development from acetate. It has similar properties to acetate, but is harder wearing and easier to wash. It can also be permanently pleated, and it resists creasing, stretching and shrinking as well as soiling. Triacetate yarns are woven into many types of fabrics, can also be knitted and are used in blends with many other fibres. Triacetate fabrics are used for a wide range of clothes and bedding, and also as a washable filling for quilts and quilted material. If articles are to be dry cleaned, special processes have to be employed (*see* Dry Cleaning, p. 24). Hand wash permanently pleated garments (unless the manufacturer states otherwise), and do not wring, twist or rub. For other articles use process $\boxed{\frac{6}{40}}$. Press, if necessary, with a cool iron, when material is damp, taking care to avoid seam impressions.

Tricel   *see* triacetate.

Tricelon   A blend of Tricel and Celon (nylon). This gives a range of lighter fabrics.

Velvet   A cut-pile fabric, made originally from silk but now from viscose, nylon and other fibres. Velvet is used for dresses and skirts, and heavier qualities are available for soft furnishings. Heavier velvets and silk or viscose velvet should be dry cleaned. Nylon velvet (and velvets guaranteed washable) can be hand washed. Do not squeeze, rub or wring. Hang to dry dripping wet, shake while drying and smooth in the direction of the pile. Velvets do not need pressing. If the pile becomes crushed, it can be raised by brushing gently or by steaming. When cutting out use a 'With Nap' layout. For a rich colour let the nap run upwards, but downwards for longer wear. Use a long machine stitch and machine in the direction of the pile; avoid top-stitching.

Vincel   A British brand name for viscose (*q.v.*).

Viscose   Rayons are the most widely used man-made fibres in the world. They are made from wood pulp, and new varieties are continually being introduced. Viscose is the most widely used. (Acetate is, strictly speaking, a rayon, but is now regarded as a separate fibre.) Viscose is similar to, but not as tough as, cotton. It is highly absorbent, it dyes well and it handles and drapes well. It is mothproof and has non-static properties. Most viscose is reasonably strong when dry, but tends to become weaker when wet. It should be handled gently during washing. Modern finishing methods have done much to overcome this problem.

Viscose is made up into many types of fabric, and is blended with almost every other fibre. It is used for clothing, many household textiles and carpets. Wash using process $\boxed{\frac{2}{60}}$, $\boxed{\frac{4}{50}}$ or $\boxed{\frac{5}{40}}$ depending on the finish, but if washing by hand do not stretch, twist or handle roughly. Iron while still damp with a warm iron. Press shiny-faced viscose on the right side, dull or matt-finished viscose on the wrong side. Never press over a seam. Sew as acetate (*q.v.*).

Viyella   A brand name for a fabric made from 55% wool and 45% cotton. Very similar to Clydella (*q.v.*).

Vyrene   A British brand name for an elastomeric fibre (*q.v.*).

Winceyette   Similar to flannelette (*q.v.*) but lighter.

Wonder-Lastic   Brand name for an elastomeric fibre (*q.v.*).

Wool   This is the hair from sheep, lambs, goats, etc., which can be spun and then woven, knitted or felted into fabric. It is absorbent, warm and soft, and has high elasticity and resilience. **Worsted** is smooth surfaced, and is made from long wool fibres. Worsted cloth is strong and hard-wearing; gaberdine and serge are worsteds. **Woollen** yarns are constructed from both long and short fibres, making a denser, hairier yarn. Woollen fabrics are warmer and softer than worsteds, but are not as durable. Moths attack wool. Wool shrinks and becomes felted and matted if handled roughly when wet. These disadvantages can be overcome by modern finishing processes.

Wool is used for a wide range of garments, for knitting yarns, and for blankets and carpets. It is blended with other fibres. Many of these modern blends, and specially treated wools, are extremely easy to care for and can be washed in a washing machine using process $\boxed{\frac{6}{40}}$ or $\boxed{\frac{7}{40}}$. Unless the manufacturer's instructions say otherwise, worsted or woollen fabrics should be dry cleaned. Knitted garments should be washed carefully by hand; do not squeeze, twist or wring, but a spin drier can be used for a short period. Do not hang up very wet garments as they will stretch out of shape. White woollens must be dried away from all heat, including sunlight, or they may discolour. Press knitted garments when dry, or nearly dry, on the wrong side, with a warm iron or a steam iron. Sewing light and medium weight wools is straightforward; to sew heavier weights needs tailoring experience.

Fabric Finishes

Many fabrics can be given special properties by finishing processes. These make them easier to care for, e.g. crease-resistant; improve them for a particular use, e.g. shower-proof; or prevent damage, e.g. mothproof, flame-resistant. Washing instructions should be adhered to exactly, or the finish may be impaired or destroyed. If the article is to be dry cleaned, the dry cleaner should be told which finish has been applied.

The following list shows some of the finishes which are used today.

Crease-resistant: Tebilized, Bancare, Minicare, Calpreta.

Shrink-resistant: Sanforized, Rigmel, Dylan, Tebilized.

Minimum-care, Drip-dry, Non-iron (intended to *reduce* the ironing needed): Sanforized Plus, Sironising, Tebilized Double Tested.

Permanent-pleating: Si-Ro-Set, Immacula.

Durable press: Koratron, Fixaform, Tootaprest, Evaprest.

Showerproof, Stain-resistant, Water-resistant:
Duracour, Scotchguard, Aqua 5.

Flame-resistant: Proban, Timonox, Fireguard, Teklan.

Mothproof: Dielmoth, Mitin.

Bacteria-resistant: Sanitized, Durafresh.

Glazed: Everglaze.

Soil-resistant: Permalose.

Anti-static: Zelac, Glencoe.

LAUNDERING

Most garments and fibres available today are supplied with cleaning instructions. These instructions are given in the form of 'The International Textile Care Labelling Code'.

If there are no instructions, but the constituent fibre is known, follow the advice given in the Chapter on **Fibres and Fabrics**.

When there is no label, and the fibre content is unknown, follow the advice below.

Wash the garment by hand in warm water (about 40°C), using a mild detergent and handling very gently. Rinse carefully, without wringing, in cool water, then finally in cold water. Give a short spin or roll in a dry towel to remove excess water; dry away from direct heat. If smoothing is necessary, press on the wrong side with a cool iron, raising the temperature to warm if needed.

Always use an iron with care.

Ironing implies a to-and-fro action which can be used on linen, cotton and other firmly woven fabrics.

Pressing means that the iron is pressed on to the material and then lifted, without moving the iron about, which may distort the fabric. Pressing should be done on the wrong side where possible, and a cloth used between the iron and the fabric. Too high a temperature can ruin a fabric, so if in doubt test, and remember that after plugging in it takes several minutes for the iron to reach the required temperature.

The International Textile Care Labelling Code

This code is issued in the United Kingdom by the Home Laundering Consultative Council (HLCC).

The code is based on four symbols. These will be found on the label of an article, or should be provided with fabric bought by the metre.

⊔ Wash tub: The Washing process.

△ Triangle: Chlorine bleaching.

⊿ Iron: Ironing.

○ Circle: Dry Cleaning.

Washing Processes

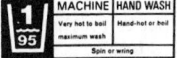 White cotton and linen articles without special finishes.

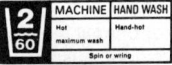 Cotton, linen or viscose articles without special finishes where colours are fast at 60°C.

 White nylon; white polyester/cotton mixtures.

 Coloured nylon; polyester; cotton and viscose articles with special finishes; acrylic cotton mixtures; coloured polyester/cotton mixtures.

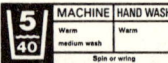 Cotton, linen or viscose articles where colours are fast at 40°C, but not at 60°C.

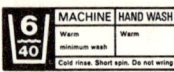 Acrylics; acetate and triacetate, including mixtures with wool; polyester/wool blends.

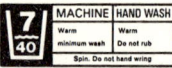 Wool, including blankets and wool mixtures with cotton or viscose; silk.

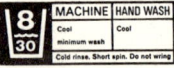 Silk and printed acetate fabrics with colours not fast at 40°C.

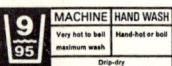 Cotton articles with special finishes capable of being boiled but requiring drip drying.

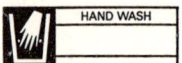 Articles which must not be machine washed. Details will vary because garment manufacturers are free to put their own written instructions on this label.

 Do not wash.

General cautionary instructions. If required, these are added to the label and kept to a minimum, e.g. dry flat, remove trimmings.

22

Ironing

There are four variations of the ironing symbol. The first three have dots to indicate variations in temperature and the fourth, the symbol crossed out, indicates that the article should not be ironed. The temperatures shown are the maximum sole plate temperatures indicated by the dots in the symbol.

hot (210°C)   Cotton, linen, viscose or modified viscose.

warm (160°C)   Polyester mixtures, wool.

cool (120°C)   Acrylic, nylon, acetate, tri-acetate, polyester.

do not iron (This symbol should only be used in cases where ironing would be detrimental to the fabric and NOT on easy care fabrics to indicate that ironing is not necessary.)

Note : formerly the setting on irons were as follows

4	hot (200°C)	Cotton, linen.
3	medium hot (180°C)	Viscose.
2	warm (150°C)	Acetate, nylon, polyester, polyester mixtures, wool.
1	cool (100°C)	Acrylic.

Chlorine Bleaching

A triangle containing the letters Cl indicates that the article may be treated with chlorine bleach. If it is crossed out this means that chlorine bleach must not be used. The symbol refers to chlorine bleach only and does not apply to other types of bleach. It is more likely to appear on the labels of European products rather than on labels of British products.

Dry Cleaning

Letters placed in a circle indicate that the article may be dry cleaned and which type of solvent may be used. Only the letters A, P and F are recognized. In some circumstances the circle containing P or F may be underlined. This indicates that special procedures are required as these goods are sensitive to dry cleaning.

(A) = Normal goods dry cleanable in all solvents.

(P) = Normal goods dry cleanable in perchloro-ethylene, white spirit, Solvent 113 and Solvent 11.

(F) = Normal goods dry cleanable in white spirit or Solvent 113.

⊠ = Do not dry clean.

STAIN REMOVAL

As far as possible, **treat a spot or stain immediately**. Before a stain has soaked in and dried, it is often possible to remove it easily and completely.

Non-greasy stains: sponge off surplus, taking care not to rub the stain in any more. Then use cool, not hot water. Immerse washable fabrics and rinse repeatedly until stain disappears. For non-washables, or where immediate immersion is not practicable, sponge gently.

Grease marks: sprinkle with talcum powder or use carbon tetrachloride on the dry fabric.

Fruit or wine stain: spread salt to prevent it spreading— but not on a carpet.

Unless laundering or the use of hot water is given as a remedy, treat the stain according to the list of methods of removal, as washing or hot water might set the stain. Several applications of a weak solution are better than one strong one. **Test all chemicals first** on an inconspicuous part of the fabric to ensure that the chemical won't damage the fabric. This applies particularly to carpets, viscose, acetates, triacetates and delicate or coloured fabrics. Never apply a second stain remover until the first has dried out and the fabric has been well rinsed with water.

When treating a stain, work from the wrong side of the material where possible. Start applying the solvent in a ring round the stain and work towards the centre, to avoid leaving a ring after the stain is removed. Rinse all chemicals out thoroughly to avoid damage. When treating carpets, take care not to saturate the carpet and do not allow the carpet backing to get wet.

Stain Removers

Stain removers should be:

Handled with care
Kept well out of the reach of children
Kept away from open fires, cookers and naked lights

Acetone   Never use on an acetate material, and test first on coloured fabrics. (Amyl acetate can be used as an alternative.) Use carefully as it is highly inflammable.

Ammonia   Use a solution of 1 tablespoonful to $\frac{1}{2}$ litre (1 pint) of warm water. If the solution affects the colour of the fabric, neutralize immediately with a weak solution of white vinegar in water, then rinse thoroughly. Ammonia gives off an overpowering gas, so use in a well-ventilated room. Cloudy ammonia is ammonia with a very small amount of soap.

Biological washing powder   For this to be effective, the fabric must soak in the solution for at least 15 minutes, which is only possible for some fabrics. As a general rule, garments needing a washing process of $\boxed{\frac{1}{95}}$, $\boxed{\frac{2}{60}}$, $\boxed{\frac{3}{60}}$ or $\boxed{\frac{9}{95}}$ can be soaked, $\boxed{\frac{4}{50}}$ and $\boxed{\frac{5}{40}}$ can sometimes be, but $\boxed{\frac{6}{40}}$, $\boxed{\frac{7}{40}}$, $\boxed{\frac{8}{30}}$, and garments which should be hand-washed only, should not be soaked. (*See* Washing Processes, p. 21).

Bleach   Household bleach (sodium hypochlorite)—well diluted—can be used only on white cotton or linen, but the milder hydrogen peroxide can be used on any fabric except nylon and some types of viscose; use 1 part of 20-volume peroxide to 6–9 parts of warm water. Rinse thoroughly.

Bleach must not dry on the material as it may damage the fibres. Do not use bleach on any garment labelled 'dry clean only'.

Borax   Use a solution of 1 dessertspoonful borax to $\frac{1}{4}$ litre ($\frac{1}{2}$ pint) warm water, and soak the stained fabric if possible; otherwise sponge. For a fresh stain, stretch the fabric over a basin, sprinkle borax over the mark, and pour boiling water through. Rinse and launder. For a large, strong stain dampen, rub in the borax and leave for half an hour, then rinse.

Detergents   These may contain soap or be soapless or synthetic. Where soap may have an adverse effect on a stain, a synthetic detergent should be used. For non-washable fabrics, use the lather only. (Make a strong detergent solution and work up a good lather with a whisk, or by repeatedly squeezing a sponge in the solution.) Always dissolve the detergent completely before immersing the material. (Never sprinkle detergent directly on to the fabric). Rinse thoroughly.

Glycerine   This acts as a lubricant and it loosens the stain. Rub in and leave for half an hour to an hour. Rinse out well or a mark will be left.

Grease solvents   These include **carbon tetrachloride, benzene, cleaning benzine, petrol, turpentine substitute (white spirit)** and **proprietary dry cleaning fluids**. They give off dangerous, inflammable fumes, so use in a well-ventilated room. Do not smoke and do not drink alcohol just before, during or just after using them. Avoid contact with the skin. A dry cleaning fluid must not be used on plastics or waterproofed material. Do not work on a plastic-laminated surface. Do not use an iron to dry solvent-wet fabric; allow the fabric to dry by evaporation.

'Hypo' (sodium thiosulphate) To use, dissolve a heaped teaspoonful in ½ litre (1 pint) warm water, soak the stain for a few seconds, rinse well and launder.

Methylated spirit Test before using on viscose. Use undiluted and sponge, or soak a bad stain. Rinse.

Oxalic acid This is **very poisonous**. It must not be used on silk, wool or viscose. Use a solution of ½ teaspoonful of crystals to ¼ litre (½ pint) water.

Vinegar Use 1 part to 4 parts water.

Refer to notes on Stain Removers (pp. 26–28) and read manufacturer's instructions.

Stain Removal Methods

Acid   Weak alkaline solution: 1 teaspoonful of washing soda or borax in $\frac{1}{2}$ litre (1 pint) warm water, or diluted ammonia (not on carpets). Rinse well.

Adhesives   It is important to remove adhesives before they dry, or they may be almost impossible to dislodge. **Glue:** For washables, use very hot water with a little detergent; for severe stains, soak in warm white vinegar for a few minutes. For non-washables, sponge with warm water, then warm white vinegar if necessary. **Water-based adhesives**: Use water, hot if the adhesive has started to dry. **Latex adhesive**; Manufacturer's special solvent. **Other adhesives**; Amyl acetate, turpentine substitute or manufacturer's special solvent. (Epoxy resin is impossible to remove once dry.)

Alcohol   Detergent or borax.

Alkali   Vinegar or vinegar solution. Rinse.

Ballpoint ink   Methylated or surgical spirit.

Balsa cement   Methylated spirit.

Beer   Launder in very hot water if possible. Otherwise use vinegar and rinse well. Use bleach on stubborn stains.

Bird droppings   *as* Faeces.

Blackberry juice   Do not use soap before neutralizing or diluting stain. Otherwise *as* Cocoa.

**Refer to notes on Stain Removers (pp. 26–28)
and read manufacturer's instructions.**

Blacklead   Turpentine substitute.

Blood   As soon as possible soak in cold, salt water. Use biological washing powder for washables; ammonia, followed by vinegar if necessary, for non-washables. Use bleach on stubborn stains.

Bottled sauce   Glycerine.

Candle wax   'Set' wax with an ice cube. Scrape off excess. Place sheets of blotting paper over and under stain, and press with warm iron. Remove any remaining colour with methylated spirit.

Carbon paper   Methylated spirit.

Cellulose lacquer   Acetone or nail-varnish remover, or amyl acetate on acetate or doubtful fabrics.

Chewing gum   Soften with carbon tetrachloride or methylated spirit. Pick off.

Chocolate   Grease solvent fluid, then *as* Cocoa.

Cocoa   Use biological washing powder for washables, otherwise borax or vinegar. Use glycerine or bleach for old and stubborn stains.

Cod-liver oil   This should be dealt with immediately. Use grease solvent, then launder or use glycerine. Use hydrogen peroxide on old stains.

Coffee   *as* Cocoa.

Crayon   Grease solvent fluid first; synthetic detergent if mark remains.

Refer to notes on Stain Removers (pp. 26–28) and read manufacturer's instructions.

Cream   Use biological washing powder for washables; otherwise sponge with warm water, then use a grease solvent.

Creosote   Benzene, eucalyptus oil or carbon tetrachloride.

Curry   Grease solvent fluid. For any remaining yellow turmeric stain use ammonia, turpentine substitute or bleach.

Deodorants   Rub stain with vinegar and rinse. Use methylated spirit if stain persists.

Dye   For small areas, use methylated spirit mixed with a few drops of ammonia, or use a dye remover.

Egg   Use biological washing powder where possible. Otherwise: for egg white, sponge with warm, not hot, salt water, rinse; for yolk, use detergent lather. Use grease solvent fluid or ammonia for stubborn stains.

Emulsion paint   Sponge or soak in cold water immediately, then launder if possible. Use methylated spirit solution on both sides of a dried stain.

Enamel paint   Turpentine substitute.

Faeces   For washables, use biological washing powder. For non-washables, use cloudy ammonia solution, then vinegar solution.

Fat   *as* Grease and Oil.

Felt-tip pens   Methylated spirit.

Refer to notes on Stain Removers (pp. 26–28) and read manufacturer's instructions.

Fruit juice   *as* Cocoa.

Glue   *see* Adhesives.

Grass   Methylated spirit or eucalyptus oil.

Gravy   For washables, use biological washing powder; otherwise use grease solvent fluid.

Grease and Oil   On most fabrics use carbon tetrachloride. Launder, using biological washing powder, if possible. For black oil, tar from beaches and stubborn stains use eucalyptus oil. For dried stains on non-washables make a paste of french chalk or talcum powder and carbon tetrachloride; spread on fairly thickly. When completely dry brush off.

Hair lacquer   Warm water then methylated spirit.

Ice cream   *as* Gravy.

Indelible pencil   Methylated spirit.

Ink   For washables, rinse and wash as soon as possible; use proprietary iron mould remover; for white cotton or linen use oxalic acid; for wool, fine and man-made fabrics use lemon juice. See also ballpoint ink.

Iodine   Ammonia or 'hypo'.

Iron mould   *as* Ink.

Jam   Launder immediately if possible, or use borax or ammonia solution.

Refer to notes on Stain Removers (pp. 26–28) and read manufacturer's instructions.

Lipstick   Vaseline, eucalyptus oil or glycerine, followed by washing if possible; otherwise dab on a few drops of ammonia and rinse well. When dry, sponge with carbon tetrachloride.

Make-up   Launder if possible. Use grease solvent fluid for non-washables or stubborn stains.

Metal polish   Ammonia solution.

Mildew   Lemon juice and salt.

Milk   For washables, rinse thoroughly in cool water, then use biological washing powder. Use borax if stain persists. For non-washables, sponge with cool water then remove any remaining grease stain with a grease solvent.

Mud   Allow to dry. Brush off.

Mustard   Glycerine.

Nail varnish   *as* Cellulose lacquer.

Nicotine   Methylated spirit.

Oil   *see* Grease and Oil.

Paint   (for Cellulose lacquer, Creosote, Emulsion and Enamel paints, Varnish, *see* separate entries). Wipe up surplus immediately, then sponge oil-based paint stains with turpentine substitute or benzene.

Paraffin   Benzene, petrol or carbon tetrachloride.

Perfume   Glycerine.

Perspiration   Borax, vinegar or ammonia solution. Use biological washing powder on washable fabrics.

Port   *as* Cocoa.

Potassium permanganate   For light fabrics, sponge with solution of hydrogen peroxide and a few drops of vinegar. Where fabric is suitable, use oxalic acid.

Rust   *as* Ink.

Scorch marks   (No remedy for bad scorch marks.) Soak in cold milk immediately. Sponge or wash with warm water and borax. Rinse thoroughly.

Sealing wax   Methylated spirit.

Sea water   Use warm water to dissolve salt.

Sherry   *as* Cocoa.

Shoe polish   Grease solvent fluid. Methylated spirit to remove any remaining colour.

Soot   Grease solvent fluid.

Sun tan oil   Grease solvent. Use borax to remove any colour stain.

Tar   *see* Grease and Oil.

Tea   *as* Cocoa.

Transfers   Methylated spirit with a few drops of ammonia added.

**Refer to notes on Stain Removers (pp. 26–28)
and read manufacturer's instructions.**

Urine   For washables, neutralize stain with vinegar, then use biological washing powder. For non-washables, sponge with warm salt water with a few drops of hydrogen peroxide added.

Varnish   Methylated spirit.

Vegetable   *as* Cocoa.

Vomit   For washables, use biological washing powder; for non-washables, sponge with salt solution. Use grease solvent on any remaining stain.

Wine   *as* Cocoa.

DRESSMAKING

It is not possible within the confines of this book to provide a guide to dressmaking. The following is intended to complement the Sewing Guide provided with patterns and, with the information given in the chapter on **Fibres and Fabrics**, to help in achieving the best possible results from the multiplicity of fabrics available.

Choose a pattern with clear instructions. (See the end of this chapter for Pattern Sizes.) Pay particular attention to the 'suggested fabrics' as the pattern will have been designed for fabrics with a particular weight and draping quality. If a non-recommended fabric is used, the resulting garment will probably not hang correctly, and some of the techniques necessary to assemble it may be difficult or impossible. If alterations have to be made to the pattern, either alter the pattern pieces before using them or, when laying out and cutting out, remember to allow extra material at any seam line which may have to be moved out, or at any hem line which may have to be let down.

Grain refers to the direction of the fabric threads. It is very important to cut pattern pieces on the straight grain of the fabric. If this is not done the finished garment may hang incorrectly. A length of fabric is said to be on-grain if the lengthwise and crosswise threads run perpendicular to each other. If the fabric is off-grain it must be straightened before cutting out. This may not be possible if the fabric has a permanent finish, particularly a drip-dry finish which locks the threads together.

Without Nap refers to any material which can be cut with the pattern pieces laid either way.

With Nap means that all pattern pieces must be cut in one direction on the fabric. These 'With Nap' fabrics are not only pile or napped fabrics such as velveteen, velvet, corduroy and fur fabrics, but those which reflect light in different ways such as a satin weave, those with a one-way design and knitted fabrics. 'With Nap' layouts generally take more material than 'Without Nap' layouts.

Check that there are no imperfections in the material. If there are, try to lay the pattern pieces round them, or position the flaws in an inconspicuous place. Patterned fabrics should be cut out with an eye to the final effect; the larger the design, the more care should be taken with the positioning of the pattern pieces on the fabric. Garments made from plaids or stripes should be cut out so that the stripes match at important seams. Note that it may be necessary to buy more material than listed on the pattern envelope in order to position pieces as required.

Refer to the chapter on **Fibres and Fabrics** for characteristics of fabrics, for sewing tips and for ironing techniques and temperatures. Assemble the garment by following the Sewing Guide provided with the pattern. Before doing any machining, test the sewing machine on layers of the fabric, and adjust stitch length and tension to give a smooth line of stitches. It is most important to press seams and darts thoroughly at each stage (unless the fabric should not be ironed). Later they will become less accessible. Before pressing seams open, iron the stitching to smooth out any puckering. Baste (tack) and check for correct fit before doing any machining or pressing.

Linings, Underlinings and Interfacings

In dressmaking the correct choice of these shaping materials is most important. They should be of the correct weight, so as not to adversely affect the hang of the finished garment; their colour should match or tone with the fabric colour; they must be capable of being laundered or dry cleaned successfully with the garment; in particular there must be no shrinkage.

A **lining** serves to tidy up the inside of a garment, it adds to the life of a garment and helps it to keep its shape. A garment and its lining are made up separately, using the same pattern pieces but cutting the lining back at facings. **Underlinings** give greater protection against a garment seating, creasing or generally losing its shape. They are particularly useful in skirts or trousers to prevent bagginess and seating, in all garments made from soft, loosely woven fabrics, and for very sheer or lacy fabrics, except where a loose, floating effect is desired. The material used for the underlining should be capable of withstanding the ironing temperature that the outside fabric needs for a good finish. Underlinings are not normally used for sleeves. The underlining is cut out using the same pattern pieces as for the garment. Matching pieces of the garment and underlining are basted together, and the garment is assembled, treating the two layers as one fabric. **Linings** and **underlinings** should be assembled so that the right side shows on the inside.

Interfacings are used in collars, cuffs and facings to help maintain their shape. They may be of woven or non-woven fabric, and come in various weights. Non-woven facings such as Vilene usually carry the manufacturer's recommendation as to which weight should be used with which fabrics. Interfacings are supplied in iron-on versions, which stick to fabrics under the heat and pressure of an iron. They are suitable for *small* areas on a fabric that is not heat sensitive.

Pattern Sizes

Patterns are designed for toddlers, children, boys and men, and for various figure types for girls and women. The measurements given are actual body measurements. The garments will be larger to allow for movement.

Toddlers and Children

Toddlers' patterns are designed for the non-walking child. The patterns are based on waist and chest measurements. Select by these and not according to the age or height of the child.

Size	$\frac{1}{2}$		1		2		3		4		5		6	
	cm	in	cm	in	cm	in	cm	in	cm	in	cm	in	cm	in
Chest	48	19	51	20	53	21	56	22	58	23	61	24	64	25
Waist	48	19	50	19½	51	20	52	20½	53	21	55	21½	56	22
Hip	—		—		—		—		61	24	64	25	66	26
Back waist length	—		21	8¼	22	8½	23	9	24	9½	25·5	10	27	10½
Approx. height	71	28	79	31	87	34	94	37	102	40	109	43	117	46

Boys and Men

Select shirt sizes by neck measurement, jacket and coat sizes by chest measurement, trousers by waist measurement.

Boys   Teen-boys

Size	7		8		10		12		14		16		18		20	
	cm	in	cm	in	cm	in	cm	in	cm	in	cm	in	cm	in	cm	in
Chest	66	26	69	27	71	28	76	30	81	32	85	33½	89	35	93	36½
Waist	58	23	61	24	64	25	66	26	69	27	71	28	74	29	76	30
Hip (seat)	69	27	71	28	75	29½	79	31	83	32½	87	34	90	35½	94	37
Neck- band	30	11¾	31	12	32	12½	33	13	34·5	13½	35·5	14	37	14½	38	15
Height	122	48	127	50	137	54	147	58	155	61	163	64	168	66	173	68

Men

Size	34		36		38		40		42		44		46		48	
	cm	in	cm	in	cm	in	cm	in	cm	in	cm	in	cm	in	cm	in
Chest	87	34	92	36	97	38	102	40	107	42	112	44	117	46	122	48
Waist	71	28	76	30	81	32	87	34	92	36	99	39	107	42	112	44
Hip (seat)	89	35	94	37	99	39	104	41	109	43	114	45	119	47	124	49
Neckband	35·5	14	37	14½	38	15	39·5	15½	40·5	16	42	16½	43	17	44·5	17½
Shirt sleeve	81	32	81	32	84	33	84	33	87	34	87	34	89	35	89	35

Girls and Women

Misses'

Misses' patterns are designed for a well-proportioned and developed figure. Height about 1·65 m–1·68 m (5 ft 5 in–5 ft 6 in) without shoes. Hip, 23 cm (9 in) below waist.

Size	6		8		10		12		14		16		18		20	
	cm	in	cm	in	cm	in	cm	in	cm	in	cm	in	cm	in	cm	in
Bust	78	30½	80	31½	83	32½	87	34	92	36	97	38	102	40	107	42
Waist	58	23	61	24	64	25	67	26½	71	28	76	30	81	32	87	34
Hip	83	32½	85	33½	88	34½	92	36	97	38	102	40	107	42	112	44
Back waist length	39·5	15½	40	15¾	40·5	16	41·5	16¼	42	16½	42·5	16¾	43	17	44	17½

Women's

Women's patterns are designed for the larger, more fully mature figure. Height, about 1·65 m–1·68 m (5 ft 5 in–5 ft 6 in) without shoes. Hip, 23 cm (9 in) below waist. Long Back waist length.

Size	38		40		42		44		46		48		50	
	cm	in	cm	in	cm	in	cm	in	cm	in	cm	in	cm	in
Bust	107	42	112	44	117	46	122	48	127	50	132	52	137	54
Waist	89	35	94	37	99	39	105	41½	112	44	118	46½	124	49
Hip	112	44	117	46	122	48	127	50	132	52	137	54	142	56
Back waist length	44	17¼	44	17⅜	44·5	17½	45	17⅝	45	17¾	45·5	17⅞	46	18

Junior Petite

Junior Petite patterns are designed for a well-proportioned petite figure. Height, about 1·52 m–1·55 m (5 ft–5 ft 1 in) without shoes. Hip, 18 cm (7 in) below waist.

Size	3jp		5jp		7jp		9jp		11jp		13jp	
	cm	in	cm	in	cm	in	cm	in	cm	in	cm	in
Bust	78	30½	79	31	81	32	84	33	87	34	89	35
Waist	57	22½	58	23	61	24	64	25	66	26	69	27
Hip	80	31½	81	32	84	33	87	34	89	35	92	36
Back waist length	35·5	14	36	14¼	37	14½	37·5	14¾	38	15	39	15¼

Half-size

Half-size patterns are for a fully developed figure with a short back waist length. Waist and hip are larger in proportion to bust than other figure types. Height, about 1·57 m–1·60 m (5 ft 2 in–5 ft 3 in) without shoes. Hip, 18 cm (7 in) below waist.

Size	**10½**		**12½**		**14½**		**16½**		**18½**		**20½**		**22½**		**24½**	
	cm	*in*	cm	*in*	cm	*in*	cm	*in*	cm	*in*	cm	*in*	cm	*in*	cm	*in*
Bust	84	*33*	89	*35*	94	*37*	99	*39*	104	*41*	109	*43*	114	*45*	119	*47*
Waist	69	*27*	74	*29*	79	*31*	84	*33*	89	*35*	96	*37½*	102	*40*	108	*42½*
Hip	89	*35*	94	*37*	99	*39*	104	*41*	109	*43*	116	*45½*	122	*48*	128	*50½*
Back waist length	38	*15*	39	*15¼*	39·5	*15½*	40	*15¾*	40·5	*15⅞*	40·5	*16*	41	*16⅛*	41·5	*16¼*

Young Junior/Teen

This size range is designed for the developing pre-teen and teen figures. Height, about 1·55 m–1·60 m (5 ft 1 in–5 ft 3 in) without shoes. Hip, 18 cm (7 in) below waist.

Size	**5/6**		**7/8**		**9/10**		**11/12**		**13/14**		**15/16**	
	cm	*in*	cm	*in*	cm	*in*	cm	*in*	cm	*in*	cm	*in*
Bust	71	*28*	74	*29*	78	*30½*	81	*32*	85	*33½*	89	*35*
Waist	56	*22*	58	*23*	61	*24*	64	*25*	66	*26*	69	*27*
Hip	79	*31*	81	*32*	85	*33½*	89	*35*	93	*36½*	97	*38*
Back waist length	34·5	*13½*	35·5	*14*	37	*14½*	38	*15*	39	*15⅜*	40	*15¾*

Girls'

Girls' patterns are designed for the girl who has not yet begun to mature.

Size	7		8		10		12		14	
	cm	in	cm	in	cm	in	cm	in	cm	in
Breast	66	26	69	27	73	28½	76	30	81	32
Waist	58	23	60	23½	62	24½	65	25½	67	26½
Hip	69	27	71	28	76	30	81	32	87	34
Back waist length	29·5	11½	31	12	32.5	12¾	34·5	13¼	36	14¼
Approx. height	127	50	132	52	142	56	149	58½	155	61

Metric Conversion Tables

These tables give the standard equivalents as approved by the Pattern Fashion Industry.

Inches (in) to Millimetres (mm) and Centimetres (cm)
(slightly rounded)

inches	mm		cm
⅛	3 mm		
¼	6 mm		
⅜	10 mm	or	1 cm
½	13 mm	or	1·3 cm
⅝	15 mm	or	1·5 cm
¾	20 mm	or	2 cm
⅞	22 mm	or	2·2 cm
1	25 mm	or	2·5 cm
1¼	32 mm	or	3·2 cm
1½	38 mm	or	3·8 cm
1¾	45 mm	or	4·5 cm
2	50 mm	or	5 cm
2½	65 mm	or	6·5 cm
3	75 mm	or	7·5 cm
3½	90 mm	or	9 cm
4	100 mm	or	10 cm
4½	115 mm	or	11·5 cm
5	125 mm	or	12·5 cm
5½	140 mm	or	14 cm
6	150 mm	or	15 cm

inches	cm	inches	cm
7	18	29	73·5
8	20·5	30	76
9	23	31	79
10	25·5	32	81·5
11	28	33	84
12	30·5	34	86·5
13	33	35	89
14	35·5	36	91·5
15	38	37	94
16	40·5	38	96·5
17	43	39	99
18	46	40	101·5
19	48·5	41	104
20	51	42	106·5
21	53·5	43	109
22	56	44	112
23	58·5	45	114·5
24	61	46	117
25	63·5	47	119·5
26	66	48	122
27	68·5	49	124·5
28	71	50	127

Yards to Metres
(slightly rounded)

yards	metres	yards	metres
$\frac{1}{8}$	0·15	$3\frac{1}{8}$	2·90
$\frac{1}{4}$	0·25	$3\frac{1}{4}$	3·00
$\frac{3}{8}$	0·35	$3\frac{3}{8}$	3·10
$\frac{1}{2}$	0·50	$3\frac{1}{2}$	3·20
$\frac{5}{8}$	0·60	$3\frac{5}{8}$	3·35
$\frac{3}{4}$	0·70	$3\frac{3}{4}$	3·45
$\frac{7}{8}$	0·80	$3\frac{7}{8}$	3·55
1	0·95	4	3·70
$1\frac{1}{8}$	1·05	$4\frac{1}{8}$	3·80
$1\frac{1}{4}$	1·15	$4\frac{1}{4}$	3·90
$1\frac{3}{8}$	1·30	$4\frac{3}{8}$	4·00
$1\frac{1}{2}$	1·40	$4\frac{1}{2}$	4·15
$1\frac{5}{8}$	1·50	$4\frac{5}{8}$	4·25
$1\frac{3}{4}$	1·60	$4\frac{3}{4}$	4·35
$1\frac{7}{8}$	1·75	$4\frac{7}{8}$	4·50
2	1·85	5	4·60
$2\frac{1}{8}$	1·95	$5\frac{1}{8}$	4·70
$2\frac{1}{4}$	2·10	$5\frac{1}{4}$	4·80
$2\frac{3}{8}$	2·20	$5\frac{3}{8}$	4·95
$2\frac{1}{2}$	2·30	$5\frac{1}{2}$	5·05
$2\frac{5}{8}$	2·40	$5\frac{5}{8}$	5·15
$2\frac{3}{4}$	2·55	$5\frac{3}{4}$	5·30
$2\frac{7}{8}$	2·65	$5\frac{7}{8}$	5·40
3	2·75	6	5·50

yards	metres	yards	metres
$6\frac{1}{8}$	5·60	$8\frac{1}{8}$	7·45
$6\frac{1}{4}$	5·75	$8\frac{1}{4}$	7·55
$6\frac{3}{8}$	5·85	$8\frac{3}{8}$	7·70
$6\frac{1}{2}$	5·95	$8\frac{1}{2}$	7·80
$6\frac{5}{8}$	6·10	$8\frac{5}{8}$	7·90
$6\frac{3}{4}$	6·20	$8\frac{3}{4}$	8·00
$6\frac{7}{8}$	6·30	$8\frac{7}{8}$	8·15
7	6·40	9	8·25
$7\frac{1}{8}$	6·55	$9\frac{1}{8}$	8·35
$7\frac{1}{4}$	6·65	$9\frac{1}{4}$	8·50
$7\frac{3}{8}$	6·75	$9\frac{3}{8}$	8·60
$7\frac{1}{2}$	6·90	$9\frac{1}{2}$	8·70
$7\frac{5}{8}$	7·00	$9\frac{5}{8}$	8·80
$7\frac{3}{4}$	7·10	$9\frac{3}{4}$	8·95
$7\frac{7}{8}$	7·20	$9\frac{7}{8}$	9·05
8	7·35	10	9·15

Available Fabric Widths

25 in	65 cm	50 in	127 cm
27 in	70 cm	54/56 in	140 cm
35/36 in	90 cm	58/60 in	150 cm
39 in	100 cm	68/70 in	175 cm
44/45 in	115 cm	72 in	180 cm
48 in	122 cm		

Available Zipper Lengths

4 in	10 cm	10 in	25 cm	22 in	55 cm
5 in	12 cm	12 in	30 cm	24 in	60 cm
6 in	15 cm	14 in	35 cm	26 in	65 cm
7 in	18 cm	16 in	40 cm	28 in	70 cm
8 in	20 cm	18 in	45 cm	30 in	75 cm
9 in	22 cm	20 in	50 cm		